DUETS FOR F OR RECORDERS

MB22186

BY CLARK KIMBERLING

© 2010 BY MEL BAY PUBLICATIONS, INC., PACIFIC, MO 63069.
ALL RIGHTS RESERVED. INTERNATIONAL COPYRIGHT SECURED. B.M.I. MADE AND PRINTED IN U.S.A.
No part of this publication may be reproduced in whole or in part, or stored in a retrieval system, or transmitted in any form
or by any means, electronic, mechanical, photocopy, recording, or otherwise, without written permission of the publisher.

Visit us on the Web at www.melbay.com or www.billsmusicshelf.com

PREFACE

These seventy-five duets were arranged for several combinations: two flutes, or various pairs of recorders, such as S&A, S&T, A&T, as well as equal instruments, such as two alto recorders. The duets are all fresh – no transcriptions.

As you would expect in such a large collection, there is a great deal of variety – from easy (Horns) to advanced (Kromatiks), from Native American to Russian, from Susato to Sir Arthur Sullivan. From slow and brooding (Zantazipporah) to exuberant (Because I'm Twenty-Five); from mysterious (Cacophon) to straightforward (March). Among composers represented are Bach, Couperin, Dow, Hill, Purcell, Sullivan, and Susato.

Along with arrangements of well established melodies from around the world, more than half of the duets were composed for this collection, with careful attention to the capabilities and special characteristics of flutes and recorders.

For details, see the Contents and the Notes at the end of Contents. The duets follow a collection of more than one-thousand solos, some available on-line and others from Mel Bay Publications, as listed at the end of this book.

Many of these duets have been played at gatherings of flute choirs and large groups of recorders. For such use, doublings of parts, sometimes at an octave, work quite well. For Feel free to add piccolos, sopranino recorders, and bass recorders.

CONTENTS

Arpegge 1
2 flutes, or recorders: AT   Clark Kimberling   7

Arpegge 2
2 flutes, or recorders: AT   Clark Kimberling   8

Baraq
2 flutes, or recorders: AT   Clark Kimberling   10

Because I'm Twenty Five
2 flutes, or recorders: ST   Faustina H. Hodges   12

Bounce
2 flutes, or recorders: TT, SS, ST   Clark Kimberling   14

Butterfly You Painted Has Flown, The
2 flutes, or recorders: TT, AT, ST   Pueblo Indian Melody   16

Cacaphon
2 flutes, or recorders: TT   Clark Kimberling   18

Cartesia
2 flutes, or recorders: AT   Clark Kimberling   19

Chatter
2 flutes, or recorders: SA   Clark Kimberling   20

Damalia
2 flutes, or recorders: AT   Clark Kimberling   22

Desert Bee
2 flutes, or recorders: AT   Clark Kimberling   24

Essence of Old Kentucky
2 flutes, or recorders: ST   American Melody   26

Fais Do-Do
2 flutes, or recorders: TT, SS, ST   Creole Folk Melody   28

Fanfare in D
2 flutes, or recorders: SS, TT, AT   Clark Kimberling   30

Fillienne
2 flutes, or recorders: AT   Clark Kimberling   33

Fritillaries
2 flutes, or recorders: TT, SS, AT, ST   Clark Kimberling   32

Horns
2 flutes, or recorders: TT, SS   Clark Kimberling   36

I Wish You Would Marry Me Now
2 flutes, or recorders: ST, SS, TT   Scottish Melody   38

Incanta 1
2 flutes, or recorders: AT   Clark Kimberling   40

Incanta 2
2 flutes, or recorders: AT   Clark Kimberling   42

Jeanne D'Arc
2 flutes, or recorders: ST, SS, TT   French Melody   44

Jump Little Rabbit
2 flutes, or recorders: ST   Russian Melody   46

Kromatik 1
2 flutes, or recorders: SS, TT, ST   Clark Kimberling   48

Kromatik 2
2 flutes, or recorders: AT, SS   Clark Kimberling   51
Kromatik 3
2 flutes, or recorders: ST   Clark Kimberling   52
Kromatik 4
2 flutes, or recorders: ST   Clark Kimberling   55
Kromatik 5
2 flutes, or recorders: AT   Clark Kimberling   56
La Diane
2 flutes, or recorders: ST, SS, TT   François Couperin   58
Le Tambourin
2 flutes, or recorders: ST, SS, TT   Jean-Philippe Rameau   60
Les Papillons
2 flutes, or recorders: ST, SS, TT   François Couperin   62
Lone Oak
2 flutes, or recorders: AA   Clark Kimberling   64
March
2 flutes, or recorders: SA   Johann Sebastian Bach   66
Memories
2 flutes, or recorders: TT   Clark Kimberling   68
Minuet
2 flutes, or recorders: ST, TT, SS   Henry Purcell   70
Mixo
2 flutes, or recorders: AT, SS, TT   Clark Kimberling   72
My Eyes Are Fully Open
2 flutes, or recorders: ST, TT, SS   Sir Arthur Sullivan   74
O Dear Beloved
2 flutes, or recorders: AT   Egyptian Melody   76
Octivo
2 flutes, or recorders: SS, TT, AT, ST   Clark Kimberling   78
Out and Around
2 flutes, or recorders: AT   Clark Kimberling   80
Picante
2 flutes, or recorders: TT, SS   Clark Kimberling   82
Ripplets
2 flutes, or recorders: TT, ST, SS   Clark Kimberling   84
Rondo 1
2 flutes, or recorders: SA   Tielman Susato   86
Saharia
2 flutes, or recorders: AT   Clark Kimberling   88
Sailor's Dance, The
2 flutes, or recorders: ST, TT, SS   Henry Purcell   90
Sleepy Maggie
2 flutes, or recorders: ST, TT, SS   Nathaniel Dow   92
Snowflakes
2 flutes, or recorders: ST   Mildred Jane Hill   94

Soaring
2 flutes, or recorders: AT	Clark Kimberling	95

Soprissimo
2 flutes, or recorders: SS	Clark Kimberling	96

Sprites
2 flutes, or recorders: SA	Clark Kimberling	97

There's a Reason
2 flutes, or recorders: TT, SS	Clark Kimberling	98

Tryggare Kan Ingen Vara
2 flutes, or recorders: TT	Swedish Melody	100

Wer Nur Den Lieben Gott
2 flutes, or recorders: SS, TT	Georg Neumark	102

White Swans
2 flutes, or recorders: AT, ST	Clark Kimberling	105

Whole Tone Meringue
2 flutes, or recorders: AT, ST	Clark Kimberling	106

Writhm
2 flutes, or recorders: AT	Clark Kimberling	108

Za Di Za Didi Za Za
2 flutes, or recorders: ST, SS, TT	Clark Kimberling	116

Zaccarie
2 flutes, or recorders: ST, SS, TT	Clark Kimberling	118

Zalanda
2 flutes, or recorders: ST, TT, SS	Clark Kimberling	120

Zantagertrudis
2 flutes, or recorders: ST, SS, TT	Clark Kimberling	122

Zantazipporah
2 flutes, or recorders: TT	Clark Kimberling	125

Zapacho
2 flutes, or recorders: St, SS, TT	Clark Kimberling	126

Zavalse
2 flutes, or recorders: ST, SS, TT	Clark Kimberling	128

Zestina
2 flutes, or recorders: SS, TT, ST	Clark Kimberling	130

Zestivity
2 flutes, or recorders: ST, SS, TT	Clark Kimberling	131

Zhickadee
2 flutes, or recorders: SS, ST	Clark Kimberling	132

Zhruska
2 flutes, or recorders: ST	Clark Kimberling	134

Zippa Jee
2 flutes, or recorders: ST, SS, TT	Clark Kimberling	136

Zizzle
2 flutes, or recorders: ST	Clark Kimberling	138

Zizzletta
2 flutes, or recorders: ST	Clark Kimberling	141

Zmancha
2 flutes, or recorders: ST, SS, TT	Clark Kimberling	142

Zolari
 2 flutes, or recorders: SS, TT   Clark Kimberling   144
Z'Valse 1
 2 flutes, or recorders: SS, TT, ST   Clark Kimberling   110
Z'Valse 6
 2 flutes, or recorders: SS, TT, ST   Clark Kimberling   112
Z'Valse 11
 2 flutes, or recorders: SS, TT, ST   Clark Kimberling   114
Zwinkle
 2 flutes, or recorders: ST, SS, TT   Clark Kimberling   146

Note 1. Designations like "Egyptian Melody" mean that the duet is based on a well known melody that was arranged as a duet by Clark Kimberling.

Note 2. Several of the duets, including all with names starting with the letter Z, are based on solos. For access to the solos, visit the composer's webpage

http://faculty.evansville.edu/ck6/

and scroll to Music Project 1. The solos – a total of 1837 – occupy twelve collections, beginning with African-American and Jamaican Melodies, and ending with Western European Melodies.

Note 3. Wherever TT (for 2 tenor recorders) occurs, the duet may be played on alto recorders using C-fingering.

Note 4. Recorder glissando is indicated by a straight segment between two notes, as in measure 19 of "Bounce." Flutes may substitute a slur or fingered glissando.

Note 5. Designations like "ST, SS, TT" indicate possible combinations of two recorders. Other combinations are possible, and, in particular, there are ample opportunities for the use of sopranino and bass recorders.

Note 6. Consider each duet to be a trio in which the third instrument is the acoustics of the space in which the duet is played. The acoustical environment is very important.

Two flutes or recorders: A & T

ARPEGGE 1

Clark Kimberling

Two flutes or recorders: A & T

ARPEGGE 2

Clark Kimberling

8

Two flutes
or recorders: A & T

BARAQ

Clark Kimberling

Two flutes or recorders: TT or AT or ST

THE BUTTERFLY YOU PAINTED HAS FLOWN AWAY

Pueblo Indian Melody
arr. Clark Kimberling

Two flutes or recorders: T & T

CACOPHON

Clark Kimberling

Two flutes or recorders A & T

CARTESIA

Clark Kimberling

Two flutes or recorders: A&T

DAMALIA

Clark Kimberling

Two flutes or recorders: A&T

DESERT BEE

Clark Kimberling

Indiana University Hospital
Dec. 25, 2009

Indiana University Hospital
Dec. 25, 2009

Two flutes or recorders: TT, SS, AT, ST

FRITILLARIES

Clark Kimberling

Two flutes
or recorders: TT or AT or SS

HORNS

Clark Kimberling

*This page has been left blank
to avoid awkward page turns.*

Two flutes or recorders: A & T

INCANTA 1

Clark Kimberling

Two flutes or recorders: A&T

INCANTA 2

Clark Kimberling

*This page has been left blank
to avoid awkward page turns.*

Two flutes
or recorders: ST or SS or TT

JEANNE D'ARC

French Melody
arr. Clark Kimberling

Two flutes
or recorders: SS or TT or ST

KROMATIK 1

Clark Kimberling

48

KROMATIK 3

Clark Kimberling

Two flutes
or recorders: ST or SS or TT

KROMATIK 4

Clark Kimberling

Two flutes or recorders: ST or SS or TT

LA DIANE

François Couperin
arr. Clark Kimberling

Two flutes or recorders: T & T

MEMORIES

Clark Kimberling

Two flutes or recorders: AT or SS or TT

MIXO

Clark Kimberling

Two flutes or recorders: ST, TT, SS

MY EYES ARE FULLY OPEN

Arthur Seymour Sullivan
arr. Clark Kimberling

Two flutes or recorders: A & T

O DEAR BELOVED

Egyptian Melody
arr. Clark Kimberling

Two flutes or recorders: SS or TT or AT or ST

OCTIVO

Clark Kimberling

78

Two flutes or recorders: A & T

OUT AND AROUND

Clark Kimberling

Two flutes
or recorders: TT or SS

PICANTE

Clark Kimberling

Two flutes
or recorders: TT or ST or SS

Clark Kimberling

RIPPLETS

Two flutes
or recorders: A&T

SAHARIA

Clark Kimberling

88

93

SNOWFLAKES

Two flutes or recorders: S & T

Mildred Jane Hill
arr. Clark Kimberling

The composer of this melody, Miss Hill, of Louisville, Kentucky, also composed the world's most often sung tune. Both "Snowflakes" and the Happy Birthday tune were first published in 1893 in a collection of kindergarten songs.

Two flutes or recorders: A & T

SOARING

Clark Kimberling

Two flutes or recorders: S & S

SOPRISSIMO

Clark Kimberling

Fingerings for very high notes on soprano recorder:
G, (L2, R2);   F#, (L3, R3);   E, (L3)

Two flutes or recorders: S & A

SPRITES

Clark Kimberling

♩ = 100
Always heavily accent downbeats.
simile

Two flutes
or recorders: TT or SS

THERE'S A REASON

Clark Kimberling

98

Two flutes or recorders: T & T

TRYGGARE KAN INGEN VARA

Swedish Melody
arr. Clark Kimberling

Indiana University Hospital
Dec. 25-26, 2009

Two flutes or recorders: AT or ST or AT

WHITE SWANS

Clark Kimberling

Two flutes
or recorders: AT or TT or ST

WHOLE TONE MERINGUE

Clark Kimberling

109

Two flutes or recorders: SS or TT or ST

Z'VALSE 1

Clark Kimberling

Two flutes
or recorders: ST or TT or SS

Z'VALSE 11

Clark Kimberling

Two flutes,
or recorders: ST or SS or TT

ZA DI ZA DIDI ZA ZA

Clark Kimberling

Two flutes, or recorders: ST or TT or SS

ZALANDA

Clark Kimberling

subito swing style

(swing)

Two flutes,
or recorders: ST or SS or TT

ZANTAGERTRUDIS

Clark Kimberling

Two flutes or recorders: T & T

ZANTAZIPPORAH

Clark Kimberling

125

Two flutes, or recorders: ST or SS or TT

ZAPACHO

Clark Kimberling

Two flutes,
or recorders: ST or TT or SS

ZAVALSE

Clark Kimberling

Two flutes or recorders: SS or TT or ST

ZESTINA

Clark Kimberling

Two flutes or recorders: ST or SS or TT

ZESTIVITY

Clark Kimberling

131

Two flutes
or recorders: SS or ST

ZHICKADEE

Clark Kimberling

Two flutes
or recorders ST or TT or SS

ZHRUSHKA

Clark Kimberling

Two flutes or recorders: S & T

ZIPPA JEE

Clark Kimberling

*Fingerings for very high notes on soprano recorder:
G, (L2, R2);   F#, (L3, R3);   E, (L3)

137

Two flutes or recorders: SS or ST or TT

ZIZZLE

Clark Kimberling

139

Two flutes or recorders: S & T

ZIZZLETTA

Clark Kimberling

Two flutes or recorders: SS or TT

ZOLARI

Clark Kimberling

144

Two flutes
or recorders: ST or SS or TS

ZWINKLE

Clark Kimberling

BOOKS BY CLARK KIMBERLING

RECORDER

Title	ISBN
African-American & Jamaican Melodies (MB20977)	978-078666204-3
Christmas Carols for Recorder or Flute (MB20978)	978-078666197-8
Irish Melodies (MB20979)	978-078666201-2
American Melodies to 1865 (MB21229)	978-078667368-1
American Melodies after 1865 (MB21230)	978-078667369-8
British Melodies (MB21469)	978-078667583-8
Melodies by Women Composers (MB21675)	978-078668103-7
Easter European & Jewish Melodies (MB21676)	978-078668104-4

FLUTE

Title	ISBN
African-American & Jamaican Melodies (MB21696)	978-078667005-5
Christmas Carols for Recorder or Flute (MB20978)	978-078666197-8
Irish Melodies (MB22010)	978-078666105-1
American Melodies to 1865 (MB22011)	978-078668106-8
American Melodies after 1865 (MB22012)	978-078668107-5
British Melodies (MB22013)	978-078668108-2
Melodies by Women Composers (MB22014)	978-078668109-9
Easter European & Jewish Melodies (MB22015)	978-078668110-5